A POCKETFUL OF
PYTHON

PICKED
BY
ERIC
IDLE

WITH A PREFACE BY TERRY JONES
AND A FOREWORD BY THE LATE
GRAHAM CHAPMAN

methuen

WRITTEN AND CONCEIVED BY
GRAHAM CHAPMAN, JOHN CLEESE
TERRY GILLIAM, ERIC IDLE
TERRY JONES AND MICHAEL PALIN

DESIGN BY KATY HEPBURN AND ALUN EVANS

Co-ordinating editor for the *Pocketful of Python* series: Geoffrey Strachan
The texts included in this volume are taken from the film screenplays for *Monty Python and the Holy Grail, The Life of Brian* (with *Montypythonscrapbook*) and *The Meaning of Life*, published by Methuen in 1977, 1979, and 1983; *Monty Python's Big Red Book* (Methuen 1971); *The Brand New Monty Python Bok*, published in paperback as *The Brand New Monty Python Papperbok* (Methuen 1973 and 1974); and the record album/CD *The Monty Python Matching Tie and Handkerchief* (1973)

Published by Methuen 2002
10 9 8 7 6 5 4 3 2 1
First published in Great Britain by
Methuen Publishing Limited, 215 Vauxhall Bridge Road, London SW1V 1EJ

In the same series

A Pocketful of Python picked by Terry Jones
A Pocketful of Python picked by John Cleese
A Pocketful of Python picked by Michael Palin
A Pocketful of Python picked by Terry Gilliam

Methuen Publishing Limited Reg. No 3543167
A CIP catalogue record for this title is available from the British Library

ISBN 0 413 76010 3
Printed and bound in Great Britain by Butler and Tanner Ltd, Frome, Somerset

FOR
GEORGE
AKA MR PAPADOPOULOS

WITH LOVE FROM
JOHN, MICHAEL, TERRY, ERIC
TERRY AND GRAHAM

A PREFACE BY
TERRY JONES

It is a great honour to have the privilege of writing this Preface for a book the contents of which have been selected by Eric Idol. Eric first came into my life when I was three months old. He had not been born at the time, but was able to communicate via the amniotic fluid in a simple version of morse code that he had developed. The first message I remember receiving from him informed me that, when he got out, he was expecting a Porsche. A month later he amended this and told me that if I thought a mere motor car was going to tempt him out of the womb, I had another think coming. He was, his message said, quite content to stay where he was.

Eight months later I received another communication from Eric. It was full of pain and outrage. Things, it appeared, were not going well between his mother and himself. He had a dreadful feeling that she was, in some way, 'trying to expel him', as he put it, but that he was going to do his damnedest to 'stick in there'.

The next time I heard from Eric, it was via a boiled egg that he had managed to smuggle into a shopping basket belonging to a local chiropodist that my father used. It turned out that Eric had lost his earlier struggle with his genetrix, but was now reconciled to a life outside the womb, as long as the Porsche turned up, which it hadn't done so far.

I e-mailed back to say that, while I sympathised, I thought an Aston Martin might be a more suitable compensation for having to live in the real world. This was, remarkably, the first time that e-mail had been used. But, in 1944, there was no way Eric could have picked the message up. And so it was that our correspondence dwindled to a mere trickle during the post-war era of Clement Attlee, Nye Bevan and the great egg shortage of 1944–1947.

Eric would send a trickle. I would reply with an even smaller trickle. Eric would respond with several trickles and a runny bit. I would return a big trickle and a wet patch and so on and so forth. None of it meant much to either of us, but it was a comfort to know that neither of us was the only one with a weak bladder.

The truth is that Eric has always been an innovative and original communicator – one has only to think of his attempt to send messages across the Hackney Marshes by re-arranging the drainage channels so that they spelt out the first letters of the word chloroplast, or his release of lizards into the sewage system of Manhattan, in which each lizard had tied round its neck a message to one of the Beverly Sisters.

And he has remained an extraordinary communicator to this day. Why only yesterday a huge boulder, measuring 60ft in diameter, fell off my roof – crushing me to death. On the boulder in clearly chiselled Bodoni Light was the message: 'Oops! Sorry! – love Ratty'.

I shall miss Eric and our correspondence, but, being dead, I can't get too upset about it. And besides, it is enough to know that this magnificent book – a truly worthy and delightful memorial of those Golden Days behind the bicycle sheds, when a pack of ten Weights Woodbines only cost a year's wages, and all wellington boots had holes in – is now safely in your hands.

I hope, that through the medium of this volume, Eric will continue to communicate with you in the same spiritual and essentially daffy way that he has communicated with me throughout our lives and beyond.

T. J. October 2002

ABOUT **THE EDITOR**

Eric Idle was the nicest of the six members of Monty Python. He was born in the North of England well when I say the nicest he wasn't *absolutely* the nicest. Michael Palin is generally recognized as being the nicest. Actually Terry Jones is pretty nice too, and certainly he's very nice at parties. It's probably fair to say that he is at least as nice as Michael Palin at parties. Come to think of it Terry Gilliam can be fairly nice as well. Especially abroad. In fact he is super nice abroad. Perhaps almost too nice. That Graham Chapman was a nice man and even John Cleese is a lot nicer than he used to be. In fact I'd stick my neck out and say that nowadays John Cleese is probably amongst the nicest of them all. So, Eric Idle is the *sixth* nicest member of the old Monty Python group. He was born in the North of England, what's so great about being nice anyway? Many fine people have lived richly fulfilling lives without having to worry about being nice. Nobody said Mozart was 'nice'. They didn't say 'I loved Shakespeare's *Hamlet* but what a nice guy he is.' In fact many great artists weren't very nice at all. So let's just agree to leave the nice thing to one side. Eric Idle, while not being necessarily the nicest of the Monty Python group was born in the North of England during World War Two. He went to a not particularly nice boarding school in Wolverhampton from the age of seven. That's not going to make anyone very nice is it? He attended Nice College, Cambridge, oh all right *Pembroke* College, Cambridge, and became President of the Footlights (just like Peter Cook and no one ever accused *him* of being nice did they? He'd have laughed in their faces if they had. 'Don't you call me nice you daft old git' he'd have said, in that funny voice, and he'd have been absolutely right).

Eric Idle was born in the North of England and etc etc Cambridge. During the sixties and early seventies he was occasionally mistaken for Peter Cook. He now lives in California and is occasionally mistaken for Gene Wilder. He is still not particularly nice.

HOW TO TALK TO
THE QUEEN

A typical conversation with The Queen

QUEEN: Arise.

ORDINARY MAN: Thank you, your Majesty.

QUEEN: What brings you to Wolverhampton?

ORDINARY MAN: I have an aunt who lives near here – well in Wellington, actually, which is just about – (*you will have lost The Queen's attention by now. She meets many people, so keep your sentences short and sharp*).

QUEEN: Well, I must be going away . . .

ORDINARY MAN: Goodbye, your Majesty.

QUEEN: Goodbye, my man.

A bad conversation with The Queen

ORDINARY MAN: Hello, I didn't recognize you.

QUEEN: But I am The Queen!

ORDINARY MAN: You don't look at all like you do on the stamps.

QUEEN: Don't you speak to me like that, you dirty little nonentity.

ORDINARY MAN: Can you help me change this wheel?

QUEEN: Shut your fat gob, you nasty little pile of wombat's do's.

A conversation like this could ruin your chances of an O.B.E.

THE BATLEY LADIES
TOWNSWOMEN'S GUILD

President: Mrs Rita Fairbanks
Mrs Fairbanks reports on this year's production

This has been a terribly good year for the Guild. Our annual production raised more than ever and was even more popular. Thanks are due to Mrs Lowndes for doing the cakes, and of course the Vicar for the use of the field. We were the first Townswomen's Guild to put on 'Camp on Blood Island' and last year we did our extremely popular re-enactment of 'Nazi War Atrocities', so this year we decided to do something in a lighter vein. Happily we fell on 'The Battle of Pearl Harbor'. To all involved many thanks and let's hope that next year's production of 'Groupie' will be even more successful. Yours Truly,

Rita Fairbanks

Mrs Rita Fairbanks
The Dimples,
Bottomleigh,
Wainscotting,
Nr. Batley.

Mrs Rita Fairbanks and friends during rehearsals

Some previous productions
by the Batley Ladies Townswomen's Guild

1992 The Merchant of Venice

1993 Fiddler on the Roof

1994 Iolanthe

1995 Hair

1996 Salad Days

1997 Man of La Mancha

1998 Little Women

1999 Annie

2000 The Producers

2001 The Battle of Pearl Harbor

Children's Page

Hello children hello. This is Uncle Dennis welcoming you to your own page. Hello. Today we are going to have a story, so sit comfortably and we can all start.

One day, Rikki the magic Pixie, went to visit Daisy Bumble in her tumbledown cottage. He found her in the bedroom. Roughly he grabbed her heaving shoulders pulling her down on to the bed and hurriedly ripping off her thin ████████████████.

Old Nick, the Sea Captain was a rough tough jolly sort of fellow. He loved the life of the sea and he loved to hang out down by the pier where the men dressed as ladies ████████ ████████████████████ with a melon.

Rumpletweezer ran the Dinky Tinky shop in the foot of the Magic oak tree by the wobbly dum dum tree in the shade of the magic glade down in Dingly Dell. Here he sold contraceptives, ████████ and various appliances ████████ naked fun ████████ f ████ ████████ sh ███

12

THE STORY OF
THE GRAIL

*Doug and Bob are Metropolitan Policemen
with a difference*

Doug slips into a little cocktail frock while Bob bouffantes his hair for a night 'on duty'

*Chief suspects are the Brain twins (Nikky, Vance and Denise)
who torture a Mayfair trichologist into revealing, in a tender
and emotional death scene, that his hair is not his own . . .*

*Meanwhile a Kent Touring XI have trapped husky Matilda Tritt
on a 'sticky' near Hastings. She reveals all before
enforcing the follow-on*

. . . all seems to be well when suddenly, Carol, the cockney telephone sanitiser and ex-drummer for the Who, and Ronnie Medway III, tiny-brained assistant millionaire, find new love for each other in a flashback near Hastings . . .

Alas! They are trapped on the beach at Deal by Bob and Doug, disguised as the man who edited most of the Ken Russell films. Towards the end, they all kill each other and live happily ever after

SPAMELOT!

We're Knights of the Round Table
We dance whene'er we're able
We do routines and chorus scenes
With footwork impeccable
We dine well here in Camelot
We eat ham and jam and Spam a lot.

We're Knights of the Round Table
Our shows are formidable
But many times
We're given rhymes
That are quite unsingable
We're opera-mad in Camelot
We sing from the diaphragm a lot.

In war we're tough and able,
Quite indefatigable
Between our quests
We sequin vests
And impersonate Clark Gable
It's a busy life in Camelot.
SINGLE MAN: I have to push the pram a lot . . .

OH WHAT A LOVELY
DOG

Background of mouth organ and bombs falling.

OFFICER: Home on leave in two days, eh, Sarge?

SERGEANT: Yes sir.

OFFICER: Lucky man.

SERGEANT: Oh, soon be your turn sir.

OFFICER: Yes, yes, I suppose so. Is that your wife, Sarge?

SERGEANT: Yes sir.

OFFICER: You're a lucky man.

SERGEANT: You married, sir?

OFFICER: Yes, yes, rather. Did I, er, ever show you that picture of my wife, Sarge?

SERGEANT: Well, no sir.

OFFICER: Where's the damn thing? Yes, here we are. Pretty nice, eh?

SERGEANT: Oh, bit ugly though sir.

OFFICER: Ugly?

SERGEANT: You know, I mean not attractive to men, sir.

OFFICER: Well, I suppose that's rather a matter of taste, Sarge.

SERGEANT: Oh no, no she's ugly sir.

OFFICER: It's not a very good picture actually . . . it makes her nose look too big.

SERGEANT: No, the nose is all right sir, it's the eyes.

OFFICER: What's wrong?

SERGEANT: Well they're crooked sir.

OFFICER: They're not crooked.

SERGEANT: Very crooked sir.

OFFICER: Yes, yes, I s'pose so. Is that your . . . wife Sarge?

SERGEANT: No sir, that's my dog.

OFFICER: Oh. Oh. Ah . . . good looking dog, isn't it?

SERGEANT: She sir, she's a bitch.

OFFICER: *Is* she . . . ! ?

SERGEANT: Yes sir. Oh, look out sir!

Noise of bombs.

OFFICER: Er . . . Sarge . . . ?

SERGEANT: Yes sir?

OFFICER: Er . . . this dog of yours . . . quite a little stunner, isn't she?

SERGEANT: Look out sir. Oh, do you think they're bringing up the big mortars, sir?

OFFICER: Yes. Does she, er, does she have any . . . friends . . . ?

SERGEANT: What, sir?

OFFICER: Your dog.

SERGEANT: Oh, just the other dogs in the neighbourhood sir.

OFFICER: She doesn't have a . . . er . . . steady . . . er, boyfriend?

SERGEANT: Well no sir, she's a dog.

OFFICER: Yes, yes, of course.

SERGEANT: Oh . . . blimey, it's getting bad sir.

OFFICER: Yes . . . Still, I mean, she wouldn't object to someone . . . calling on her, would she Sarge?

SERGEANT: Well I'm not sure how you mean sir.

OFFICER: Er, I mean, I was thinking, perhaps I could take her for a walk some time?

SERGEANT: Oh, yes, sir, of course sir, any time.

OFFICER: Oh thank you Sarge.

SERGEANT: Look out sir! Oooh! No, that's my wife sir.

OFFICER: Are you . . . *sure* Sarge?

SERGEANT: Yes sir, that's my wife.

OFFICER: And . . . that's your dog?

SERGEANT: Yes sir.

OFFICER: I *see* . . . Look, Sarge, I think I'll be calling on you rather a lot when all this is over.

SERGEANT: Oh, thank you sir.

OFFICER: Not at all . . . it's just that I'm . . . rather fond of dogs . . .

DATE Monday

TO PYTHON

HOUR Lunc

WHILE YOU WERE OUT

M

OF The Pope called.

PHONE Vatican 6892

AREA CODE

TELEPHONED			PHONE NUMBER	
PLEASE CALL		RETURNED CALL		
WILL CALL AGAIN	✓	WAS IN		LEFT PACKAGE
		WILL RETURN		PLEASE SEE ME
				IMPORTANT

MESSAGE He said he liked the script and
would be sending you some more material.
Incidentally he explained that he was not
infallible on matters of comedy, only
when pronouncing ex-Cathedra on matters
of doctrine. He made a nice joke abou-
taking the dogma for a walk.

ALEXANDER STAT

SIGNED

(13) 464-1151

25

HOW IT ALL BEGAN–The Story of Brian

IN THE REIGN OF CAESAR AUGUSTUS THERE WENT OUT A DECREE THAT ALL THE WORLD SHOULD BE TAXED. THOUSANDS FLED INTO TAX EXILE IN JUDEA, SETTING UP OFFSHORE OVERSEAS LIMITED LIABILITY COMPANIES; AMONGST THEM, MANDY COHEN, THE MOTHER OF BRIAN, WHO WAS CARRYING THE CHILD OF NORTIUS MAXIMUS. ONE NIGHT, JUST BEFORE CHRISTMAS...

I LOVE SHEEP.

YES, SO DO I.

ME TOO. TERRIFIC ANIMALS.

NO TROUBLE.

NO, NO TROUBLE AT ALL.

EXCEPT AT SHEARING.

I LIKE THE WAY THEY GET A LITTLE BIT CROSS AT SHEARING. IT SHOWS THEY'RE HUMAN.

OH YEAH. I WASN'T SAYING I *DIS*LIKE THEM AT SHEARING, BUT THEY *CAN* BE A BIT OF A HANDFUL, CAN'T THEY?

SO WOULD *YOU* BE, IF YOU HAD A GREAT PAIR OF SCISSORS SNIPPING AWAY AT YOU WHILE SOMEBODY HELD YOUR BACK LEGS.

DON'T GET ME WRONG, MORRIS. I ACTUALLY *LOVE* SHEEP. I'D DO *ANY-THING* FOR THEM.

AND THE LITTLE LAMBS IN SPRINGTIME.

HOW IT ALL BEGAN–The Story of Brian

Oh, NOW YOU'RE TALKING. THEY'RE SO SURE-FOOTED.

AND QUICK-WITTED.

ARE THEY QUICK-WITTED?

YEAH... THEY'RE QUITE... QUICK-WITTED.

OF ALL GOD'S CREATURES, SHEEP HAVE THE FINEST OFFSPRING.

I CAN'T THINK OF ANY-THING I'D RATHER DO THAN WATCH SHEEP.

THE ONLY OTHER ANIMALS I WOULD BE REMOTELY INTERESTED IN WATCHING... WOULD BE CATS.

THEY DON'T *HAVE* FLOCKS OF CATS.

I'M NOT SAYING THEY *DO*, MORRIS.

YOU COULDN'T WATCH FLOCKS OF CATS...

CAN YOU IMAGINE... GREAT HERDS OF CATS! THEY'D BE ALL OVER THE PLACE, SCRATCHING AND BITING.

27

HOW IT ALL KEPT ON BEGINNING...

TOWARDS 0 B.C. EVERYONE GOT A LITTLE CRAZY BECAUSE THEY'D BEEN COUNTING THE YEARS BACKWARDS, AND THEY WERE RUNNING OUT OF NUMBERS. SO WHEN THEY GOT TO THE YEAR MINUS ONE, EVERYONE JUST KINDA FREAKED BECAUSE NOBODY WANTED TO REACH THE NUMBER 0, WHICH IS INFINITY. SO THEY SORTA COMPROMISED, AND SWITCHED RIGHT IN TO PLUS ONE, WHICH IS 1 A.D. (ONLY THE OTHER D. DROPPED OFF).

29

SOLLY & SARAH

SOLLY: What do you mean, the Holy Ghost?

SARAH: I said, the Holy Ghost done it.

SOLLY: He got you up the gut, the Holy Ghost did?

SARAH: Yeah.

SOLLY: You expect me to believe that the Holy Ghost took a night off from heaven, came down to number 42, Sheep Way, and shacked up with you.

SARAH: Yeah.

SOLLY: Let me get this right – the Spiritual Ruler of the entire Universe, feeling a touch randy and in need of a bit of the other, manifests himself, comes down and nips into bed with you.

SARAH: Yeah.

SOLLY: Nice one. I don't get a bit of nooky out of you for two years and next thing you're having knee tremblers with a bloody archangel.

SARAH: He's not a bloody archangel, he's the Holy Ghost.

SOLLY: Oh yeah – if the Holy Ghost climbs into bed with you – it's down with the sheets and on with the job. If it's me, it's no, not till after we're married, we must save it up it's precious.

SARAH: It's true.

SOLLY: It's so fucking precious you give it to every horny little poltergeist that comes banging on the bedroom door.

SARAH: Only one.

SOLLY: Oh only one. Sorry, not the Trinity. Three persons in one bed; no, just one sexy little seraph at a time. Sorry Solly I'm saving my cherry for a cherub.

SARAH: I couldn't turn him down, he's the Holy Ghost.

SOLLY: What did he look like, did he have his head tucked under his arm?

SARAH: He's not that sort of a ghost.

SOLLY: How do I know what sort of a ghost he is, I've not been to bed with the bugger. Madame Palm's all I get for two years, not you no, you've got your feet in the air, being humped by Heavenly visitors.

SARAH: It was spiritual.

SOLLY: If it was so spiritual how come he's left his little gift in you?

SARAH: It's a blessing.

SOLLY: I notice he doesn't stay around for the blessing. Oh no, far too busy dipping his holy wick in the lamps of foolish virgins. I mean I feel frankly, that if the Holy Ghost is going around shagging all and sundry the least he can do is stick around and see his offspring through the crêche stage.

SARAH: He said I was to tell you and you'd understand and marry me.

SOLLY: I see. I see. So my idea of the perfect wife is supposed to be someone who puts out for any dissipated sprite who fancies getting his end away with the scarlet women of the spiritual world.

SARAH: He *was* the Holy Ghost.

SOLLY: I don't care if he's the Holy Choir Invisible. I don't want any lecherous apparitions unsheathing their pork swords in my sheets.

SARAH: He was ever so nice. He said I could call him Brian.

SOLLY: Brian.

SARAH: Yes.

SOLLY: Brian, the Holy Ghost.

SARAH: Yes.

SOLLY: And do you recollect throughout two thousand years of scriptures the Holy Ghost ever being referred to previously as Brian.

SARAH: Erm no.

SOLLY: So it never crossed your mind that this smutty seraphim, this rampant genie with his pants round his ankles, might perhaps not be an angel of the most high in rut but some quite ordinary mortal with a gift of the gab and a penchant for banging underage briffit.

SARAH: I've never done it before.

SOLLY: I'm afraid my dear you've fallen for a very old line.

Pause

SARAH: Do you want me to show you what he did?

SOLLY: What?

SARAH: Do you want me to show you what he taught me?

SOLLY: What all the way? Bareback?

SARAH: I can't get more pregnant can I?

SOLLY: No.

SARAH: Somebody's got to be second.

SOLLY: Yeah.

SARAH: It's ever so nice.

SOLLY: All right.

SARAH: Between you and me, I never fancied him that much.

SOLLY: No?

SARAH: No, it wasn't very big.

SOLLY: That's not supposed to count.

SARAH: I know. But it helps.

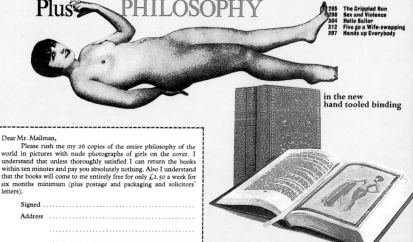

Did you know . . .

★ that El Greco's real name was E.L. Grecott?

★ **Chuck Berry wrote many of Shakespeare's plays?**

★ **the Everly Brothers turned down a knighthood?**

The Hackenthorpe Book of Lies

★ Did you know that the reason why windows steam up in cold weather is because of all the fish in the atmosphere?

★ Did you know that Moslems are forbidden to eat glass?

★ Did you know that the oldest rock in the world is the famous Hackenthorpe Rock, in North Ealing, which is 2 trillion years old?

★ Did you know that Milton was a woman?

★ Did you know that from the top of the Prudential Assurance Building in Bromley you can see 8 continents?

★ Did you know that the highest point in the world is only 8 foot?

These are just a few of the totally inaccurate facts in
THE HACKENTHORPE
BOOK OF LIES

It's all in THE HACKENTHORPE
BOOK OF LIES
A thorough and exhaustive source of misleading and untruthful information, compiled and edited by ex-Nobel Prizewinners Ron Hackenthorpe, Derek Hackenthorpe, Jeff 'The Nozz' Hackenthorpe and Luigi V. Hackenthorpe. There are 4 handsomely bound volumes, which can be purchased individually, or in our 'Pack Of Lies' gift set.

contains over 60 million untrue facts and figures.

Some highlights from
MASTURBATORS OF HISTORY

- 'Juste avant la grande bataille d'Austerlitz, et aussi les batailles d'Ulm et de Borodino, je m'avais preparé avec la main droite.' ('Before the great battle of Austerlitz and also the battles of Ulm and Borodino, I prepared myself with a quick one'). Napoleon (1813)
- George Washington (from his Diary July 1776): 'The struggle is over, the battle is won, today the independence for which we have given so much is ours by right and deed. I could never have done this without regularly twanging the wire.'
- Nansen (Norwegian Explorer): 'I find I explore better after punishing Percy in the palm.'
- Olof Palme (Swedish Prime Minister): No comment.
- Verdi: 'Composing operas is tough work, and I find the one sure way to relax is the man's way.'
- Leopold I (1640–1705): 'Being Holy Roman Emperor is tough work, you have enormous territories to defend, and in 1683 the Turks were at the gates of Vienna. I don't think I could have coped without some dirty books and a hanky.'
- Purcell (seventeenth-century English organist): 'One off the wrist keeps me in trim.'
- Michaelangelo: 'E parate di pristavere e dimmaggiore con brio Sistine marvelloso giondore.'
('Painting the roof of the Sistine Chapel is tough work. Self-abuse keeps me going').

LAVISHLY ILLUSTRATED

Masturbators of History is an entirely new way of looking at history (writes Kenneth Onan, rather shakily). For the first time we glimpse the behind-the-scenes happenings that may have influenced the course of history: the famous cross-hand during the signing of the Treaty of Utrecht, the Papal Bull making the practice compulsory during the Thirty Years War (owing to a misprint), and the reason Pilate really washed his hands. We see how it has shaped the careers of writers, musicians (especially pianists), generals and politicians. Why did Beethoven go deaf? Why was Toulouse Lautrec so small? What did Sir Walter Raleigh do in the Tower? All this and more in this fully illustrated Historical handbook. Published by Slater-Wristjob.

THE
BRUCES PHILOSOPHERS SONG

Immanuel Kant was a real pissant
Who was very rarely stable

Heidegger, Heidegger was a boozy beggar
Who could think you under the table

David Hume could out-consume
Schopenhauer and Hegel

And Wittgenstein was a beery swine
Who was just as schloshed as Schlegel

There's nothing Nietzsche couldn't teach ya
'Bout the raising of the wrist
Socrates, himself, was permanently pissed.

John Stuart Mill, of his own free will,
On half a pint of shandy was particularly ill

Plato, they say, could stick it away
Half a crate of whisky every day

Aristotle, Aristotle was a bugger for the bottle
Hobbes was found of his dram

And René Descartes was a drunken fart
'I drink, therefore I am'.

Yes, Socrates himself is particularly missed
A lovely little thinker
But a bugger when he's pissed.

CHEZ BRUCE

1. *Black Stump Bordeaux*
A peppermint-flavoured Burgundy.

2. *Sydney Syrup*
Can rank with any of the world's best sugary wines.

3. *Châteaublue*
Has won many prizes, not least for its taste, and its lingering afterburn.

4. *Old Smokey 1968*
Compares favourably with a Welsh claret.

5. *1970 Côtes du Rod Laver*
Recommended by the Australian Wino Society, this has a kick on it like a mule. Eight bottles of this and you're really finished. At the opening of the Sydney Harbour Bridge Club they were fishing them out of the main sewers every half an hour.

6. *Perth Pink*
The most famous of the sparkling wines. This is a bottle with a message in it and the message is 'Beware.' This is not a wine for drinking. It's a wine for laying down and avoiding.

7. *Melbourne Old and Yellow*
Another good fighting wine, which is particularly heavy and should be used only for hand-to-hand combat.

8. *Château Chunder*
An appellation contrôlée specially grown for those keen on regurgitation. A fine wine which really opens up the sluices at both ends.

9. *Hôbart Runny*
For real emetic fans only. Should not be served during dinner.

ASHES TO ASHES

'The Final Test' (*La Testa*)
Director Pier Paolo Pasolini
Reviewed by Clive James.

Just as Peckinpah revealed the bloodthirsty violence bubbling beneath the skin of Edwardian man, so in a different way Pasolini rips off the MCC tie to reveal the seething cauldron of sex that lies beneath the white flannels and sweaty jockstraps of today's cricketers. This is a human interest picture: the sort that makes you concentrate on the usherette. All motion picture addicts should pin back their eyeballs and take a celluloid shower in this one. It may not be exactly your cup of possum juice, but catch it if you can for the sheer magic of the Intermission which comes like a dose of clap in the middle of a mad month in a Melbourne cathouse. *The Final Test* is a movie you'd be well-advised to miss. And you'd be wrong. Go and see it. You'll be surprised. It's terrible. It's definitely Hutton dressed as Alan Lamb, but I haven't had such an

Enforcing the follow-on at Trent Bridge

enjoyable time in the cinema since I spent four hours in a Sydney
Drive-In and finally discovered it was a multi-storey car-park.
Don't miss it. Avoid it like the plague. But go anyway. You'll hate it.
It's marvellous. It's Kafka in a sheep dip, an example of the
Protestant work ethic on rollerskates, with enough acres of fresh
flesh to bring a boyish smile to the frozen features of a case-
hardened Bushman at an outback cattle auction. But enough – as
Kierkegaard observed – is a treat. Don't take your family, take
your mac. It's smashing. You'll hate it. No sweat, but all armpit.
Like sodomy, it's fun once in a while but let's hope they don't
make it compulsory. Ouch.

HOW TO
WALK SILLY

ST **BRIAN'S**

I'd like to welcome all of you parents and boys, gathered here today. As you all know, St Brian's has a tradition of homosexuality stretching back over the past five hundred years. Boys from St Brian's have always been the most sought after in Business, Industry and the Church. We have produced homosexuals of many kinds and many talents, including no less than eight gay Chancellors of the Exchequer, two very pretty heads of the Coal Board and some really outrageous old Queens who have gone into the armed forces. Many schools frown on homosexuality amongst the boys, but we at St Brian's encourage it. Boys in the sixth form can stay on and take Advanced Feeling Up, Kissing 'A' Level and Really Getting To Know Each Other right up to University standard. During the summer all the lower forms are nude. And I personally think there is no finer sight than eleven sun-drenched pairs of buttocks walking onto a cricket square on a June afternoon. The curve of a young lad's . . . I'm sorry . . . I *do* apologise, I have the wrong notes.

I'd like to welcome all of you parents and boys gathered here today. As you all know, St Brian's has a tradition of academic excellence stretching back over five hundred years. Boys from St Brian's have always been the most sought after in Business, Industry and the Church. We have produced leaders of many kinds and of many talents including eight Chancellors of the Exchequer, no less than two heads of the Coal Board and many distinguished old boys who have gone into the armed forces. St Brian himself, as the magnificent East Window of this randy old . . . of this chapel reminds us was a penis . . . a pious and god-fearing man, whose words and thoughts have been passed down to us by scholars through the centuries . . . the school fees will be going up by £50 a term as from tomorrow . . . And it is through faith in Brian and Brian's example to us that this school has prospered and whacked little boys . . . and waxed over the years. I believe there is no finer school in the lower price range. Thank you.

THE UPPER-CLASS TWIT OF THE YEAR SHOW

The Greatest Upper-Class Race in the World

1. The Start

A difficult one is this. Many of the Twits fail to get off to any kind of start whatsoever. In 1967 a Captain Brough-Oyster was a faller on his way into the stadium, and tragically had to be put down.

2. The Straight Lines

The great thing is not to take these too fast. They can be coped with more easily if the Twit imagines they are Harrods corridors.

3. The Matchbox Jump

A good Twit will take this accidentally.

4. Kicking the Beggar

The field is beginning to stagger a lot here so you can take your time. The Judge can disqualify you if you kick the Beggar after he's down more than eight times. Many great Twits have gone out at this one simply through kicking the Judge. In 1947 O. K. S. J. St. P. Semaphore went out of racing altogether when he accidentally kicked three Irish Clergy and they set about him.

5. Hunt Ball Photograph

The Twit must face the Camera. He must also try and remember to kiss the Deb and not one of the other Twits.

Now come three easier obstacles; first:

6. Reversing into the Old Lady

An easy one this for the average Twit. Also, he is for once off his own worst enemy – his feet – and into an expensive automobile. Incidentally, a firm in Surbiton supplies the old ladies.

7. Slamming the Car Door to wake the Neighbour
Second nature to Kensington dwellers. County entrants might have a little difficulty here.

8. Insulting the Waiter
Again second nature, especially if the waiter's from a proper working-class home and not just a foreigner.

9. The Bar
Perhaps the most difficult after the Debs. They must walk under the bar without braining themselves. Most take 5 or 6 goes. The winning post is in sight now as they come to the tenth.

10. Shooting the Rabbits
They are of course tied down, but this in fact makes it more difficult as it removes the chance of the animals accidentally wounding themselves.

11. Taking the Bra off the Debs
Dummies are used nowadays as occasionally the Debs got excited. It's a good idea to let your Twits see a bra before the race.

12. Shooting themselves
This requires less skill than might be imagined, for Brigadier Henry Butcher in his History of the Race claims that nearly fifty per cent of all Twits are shot accidentally by the others. Still, they all count on the scorecard, and whilst the actual winner is probably stiffening somewhere back on the Course, there's many a second and third been picked up here at the final table.

Head: look for thickness. This is what makes for outstanding Twitting. Military training is an obvious advantage here.

The Face: look for absence of expression. Is he really vacant? If he is, make for the Tote.

Tie: an important clue to breeding. MCC ties are the favourite, closely followed by Eton, Harrow and the Guards.

Watch: probably ludicrously expensive. Probably stopped.

The naughty bits: are they completely dormant? Most of them are after leaving Public School but occasionally disasters occur. Simon Main Waring Waring Main had to be pulled off one of the dummies in 1969.

Feet: the best Twits try to keep as few on the ground as possible. Rugby helps.

Balance: a good Twit should have none whatsoever.

47

KASHMIR

The expedition: it's nightfall.

WOODERSON: Look, I don't know how to say this, Bunty . . .

BUNTY: What is it Doug?

WOODERSON: Well . . . well I'm feeling so bloody randy . . .

BUNTY: Randy?

WOODERSON: Yes, damn, damn randy . . . I don't know what to do . . .

BUNTY: Whereabouts?

WOODERSON: Mm? Well . . . just all over . . . All-consuming randiness . . .

BUNTY: Well the rains'll be here soon . . .

WOODERSON: The rains . . . ?

BUNTY: Yes that should help . . .

WOODERSON: I can't seem to get my mind off it. You know . . . Bunty, just this evening, I've been trying to do some calculations for tomorrow's march and every time I open the dividers I get this damn stirring . . .

BUNTY: The dividers?

WOODERSON: Yes . . . they're a lovely wooden pair pater gave me . . . As soon as I spread them apart, Bunty . . . As soon as I open the two –

BUNTY: Yes . . . yes . . . well I think when the rains come you'll feel better . . .

WOODERSON: Bunty . . . I don't think I can wait . . . I need a . . . oh god . . . I need a woman . . .

BUNTY: Well, this is the damn problem of being in one of the most lonely, inaccessible mountain ranges on earth, Doug.

WOODERSON: What about the bearers' wives?

BUNTY: I shouldn't if I were you, Douggie . . . It's not terribly done.

WOODERSON: There *must* be women in the Kashmir . . . somewhere . . .

BUNTY: Yes . . . but not in this bit, Doug . . . this is a terribly underpopulated . . . inhospitable area . . . I mean you may find a hill-tribe that –

WOODERSON: Where? Where?

BUNTY: But if you did, Douggie . . . you must remember they're all native . . . they do things differently out here.

WOODERSON: Not what *I* want to do, Bunty . . .

BUNTY: No, there's all sorts of marriage customs and betrothal and vows. You know, women are so different out here Douglas . . .

WOODERSON: Well *men* then . . . what about men?

BUNTY: Oh Douglas! Pull yourself together . . . and wait for the rains . . .

WOODERSON: You know that tiger outside . . .

BUNTY: You're not to *touch* that tiger . . . Douglas. It's not a tiger anyway . . .

WOODERSON: It's beautiful . . .

BUNTY: It's not beautiful . . .

WOODERSON: Well the chickens then . . .

BUNTY: They're for eating, Doug . . . you know that . . .

WOODERSON: *Before* we eat them . . . ! It doesn't affect the taste . . . honestly . . .

BUNTY: Shut up. Shut up. Wait for the rains . . . like we all do. For God's sake Douglas . . . you're not the only man in Kashmir who feels randy. But this is a scientific expedition . . . don't you realise that the vegetation changes revealed by the glacial recession only occur once or twice in a lifetime . . .

WOODERSON: I know; the goat! (*he gets up*)

BUNTY: (*stands, suddenly serious, he reaches for his service revolver*) Douglas . . . leave the goat alone . . .

WOODERSON: It's so friendly . . .

BUNTY: I know it's friendly, but it's the regimental mascot, Douglas, and if you lay one finger on that goat, I will blast you off the face of this earth . . .

WOODERSON: (*provocatively*) This sounds a little more than the regimental loyalty, Bunty . . . it's only a goat . . .

BUNTY: (*blushing furiously*) Denzil is not only a goat! Denzil stands for everything that I respect.

WOODERSON: It's not your goat . . .

BUNTY: It is the regiment's goat. Denzil and I have been together for as long as I've been in the 18th Foot. I remember him when he was a tiny little goat, scarcely able to walk, and I've looked after him on every expedition since then. Scarcely a day has gone by when I haven't thought about that goat. I love him, and I love the regiment.

WOODERSON: Love; that's what I need!

(*He starts to unbutton his jacket and make for the door*)

BUNTY: Not *that* sort of love . . . Wooderson . . . you pig. I mean the higher love that can exist between two people . . . or . . . or one person and a goat . . . who respect each other . . .

WOODERSON: (*picks up a box*) May I borrow your talc?

BUNTY: Wait for the rains!

WOODERSON: I can't.

(*He pulls off his jacket, sprinkles talc under his arms, and pushes his way out of the tent.* BUNTY *goes to the tent door and fires. Then he drops his head and shakes it sadly . . . He looks up . . . worried. Then speaks sharply to the* BEARER)

BUNTY: Kanke pura . . . Wooderson dak khane lao . . .

[Fetch me Wooderson's Dividers]

Fade.

CHAOS THEORY MADE E-Z

Somewhere in the Amazon, a butterfly flaps its wings.....

... causing a storm in New York that manages to delay an airplane landing at JFK....

.... causing a banker on board to miss an International Monetary Fund meeting.....

... CAUSING A DEBATE ON THE REFINANCING OF THE BRAZILIAN NATIONAL DEBT TO FAIL....

... CAUSING THE BRAZILIAN GOVERNMENT TO COLLAPSE....

... CAUSING AN ELECTION... RESULTING IN A NEW PRESIDENT WHO BOUGHT VICTORY WITH THE PROMISE OF FREE LAND IN THE AMAZONIAN RAINFOREST FOR THE SLUM DWELLERS OF RIO...

... CAUSING ONE LUCKY BENEFICIARY NAMED JORGE TO CLAIM, AND THEN CLEAR HIS LAND IN THE MOST EFFICIENT WAY AVAILABLE ....

... CAUSING ALL THE BIRDS IN THAT ACRE OF THE FOREST TO MIGRATE DEEPER INTO THE HEART OF THE JUNGLE....

.... CAUSING AN ECOLOGICAL IMBALANCE....

... CAUSING TWO THOUSAND STARVING BIRDS TO BE WAITING AS OUR ORIGINAL BUTTERFLY IS JUST WAKING UP TO START THE ENTIRE PROCESS ALL OVER AGAIN....

THIS TIME THE BANKER MAKES HIS MEETING ON TIME.

53

If you would like to buy the film rights for this page they are still available, at least up to the point of publication they were available. Obviously if we've sold the film rights to this page since publication then they are no longer available, unless of course you make a better offer than the one we have already accepted and in that way YOU can buy the film rights to this page. We always have hidden clauses or tricky legal loopholes in our contracts in the Film Business so we can get out of things if we change our minds. So having made your offer, and we having perfectly legally dodged out of any other agreement, you can now sit back content with your new 'property' as we film people call these things.

What are you getting for your money? Well quite simply you are getting the exclusive film rights for this page IN ITS ENTIRETY, including the page number, to film in whatever manner you wish. To hire and fire directors to film this page, to go to lunch with as many screenwriters as you want and tell them exactly how to write the screenplay for this page. You can, if you want, engage film stars to appear in the screen version of this page, including Bruce Willis, Cameron Diaz, Ewan MacGregor, Billy-Bob Thornton, Steve Buscemi, Gwyneth Paltrow, or even Salma Hayek. You may then lease the distribution rights of the finished film to Warner's, or Universal or even Harrods.

So just write to Python Productions enclosing a serious cheque and we will write back and tell you if your bid has been successful or whether we have already done a deal with Harvey Weinstein. Remember, ANYONE can be a film producer, all you need is money and a certain ruthlessness. See you at the Oscars . . .

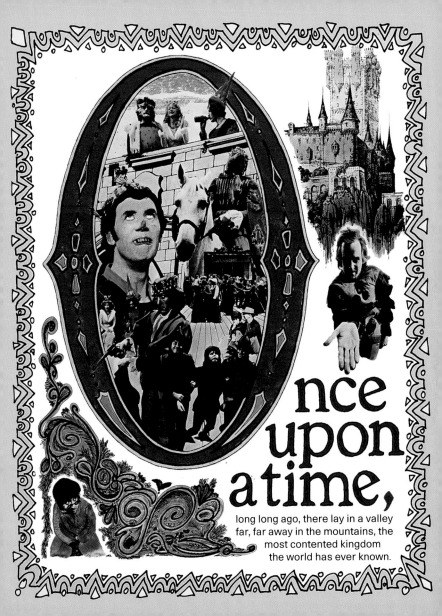

nce upon a time,

long long ago, there lay in a valley far, far away in the mountains, the most contented kingdom the world has ever known.

It was called Happy Valley, and it was ruled over by a wise old King called Otto, and all his subjects flourished and were happy, and there were no discontents or grumblers, because Wise King Otto had had them all put to death along with the Trade Union leaders many years before. And all the good happy folk of Happy Valley sang and danced all day long, and anyone who was for any reason miserable or unhappy or who had any difficult personal problems was prosecuted under the Happiness Act.

And, while the good people of Happy Valley tenaciously frolicked away, their wise old King, who was a merry old thing, played strange songs on his Hammond Organ up in the beautiful castle, where he lived with his gracious Queen Syllabub and their lovely daughter Mitzi Gaynor, who had fabulous tits and an enchanting smile, and wooden teeth which she bought in a chemist's in Augsberg, despite the fire-risk. She treasured these teeth which were made of the finest pine and she varnished them after every meal. And next to her teeth her dearest love was her pet dog Hermann. She would take Hermann for long walks and pet and fuss over him all day long and steal him tasty titbits which he never ate, because sadly he was dead and no one had the heart to tell her because she was so sweet and innocent that she knew nothing of death or gastro-enteritis or even plastic hip joints. One day, while Mitzi was taking Hermann for a pull round the Royal Gardens, she set eyes on the most beautiful young man she had ever seen and fell head over heels in love with him, naturally assuming him to be a prince.

Well, as luck would have it, he *was* a prince, and so, after looking him up in the *Observer's Book of Princes* to discover his name, she went and introduced herself and the subject of marriage, and, in what seemed like the twinkling of an eye, but was in fact a fortnight, they were on their way to see King Otto, to ask his permission to wed. What a perfect couple they looked! Mitzi, resplendent in a delicate shell-pink satin brocade and some new bullet-proof mahogany teeth, and Prince Kevin, handsome as could be, drawing many an admiring glance from some randy old closet queens in the vestibule.

Soon they were at the door of the Kingdom-Ruling Room. And then, trying to control their excitement, they were ushered into the presence of the King himself, who sat at the Royal State Organ singing his latest composition, the strangely discordant 'Ya bim dee bim, thwackety f'tang stirkel boo bum.' And when the King had finished, some hours later, and the courtiers' applause had died down, Mitzi presented Prince Kevin, who bowed gracefully and asked the wise old King for his daughter's hand in marriage.

Is he in the book?' asked the King.

'Oh yes, Daddy,' cried Mitzi.

'And do you love my daughter?' he queried, penetratingly.

'I do, sir!' replied Prince Kevin, and a ripple of delight passed round the room for already Kevin's princely bearing and sweetness of nature had won the entire court's approval.

'Good! But first, before I can grant permission, I must set you a task that you may prove yourself worthy of my daughter's hand.'

'I accept!!' cried Kevin gallantly.

The old King's face grew grave. 'At nine o'clock tomorrow morning,' he explained, 'you must go to the top of the highest tower in this castle, and armed only with your sword, jump out of the window.'

And so, early the next day, the brave young prince, dressed in a beautiful gold and white robe, and armed only with his magic sword, plummeted three hundred feet to a speedy death. How they all cheered! How funny the royal remains looked!

'Can we get married now, Daddy?' cried Mitzi, for, as we know, she knew nothing of death.

'No daughter, I'm afraid not,' answered the wise old King, although he was himself a necrophilia buff, 'he simply wasn't worthy of you.'

'Oh dear,' said Mitzi. 'Will he have to go in the ground like all the others?'

nd so most of Prince Kevin was buried alongside the remains of Prince Oswald (page 4 in the book) who'd had to fight an infantry division armed only with a copy of the *Guardian*; and Prince Robin (p. 19) who'd gallantly attempted to extinguish a fiery furnace by being thrown in it; and Prince Norbert (p. 36) who'd had to wrestle a combine harvester; and Prince Malcolm (p. 8) who'd had to catch a Boeing 747, but had dropped it.

So, the moment that Kevin's coffin had been laid to rest on the traditional huge black-edged Whoopee Cushion (for as Kevin was a prince, he had been granted a State Fancy Dress Funeral), Mitzi was off once again to the Royal Gardens, dragging the faithful Hermann behind her, to see if she could pull another prince. For princes had become extremely scarce; as rare, indeed, as an Australian virgin.

So Mitzi set off along the river bank, hopefully kissing frogs, until she spotted the slightest glint of gold from beneath a Giggling Willow Tree and running forward, espied – sure enough! – a prince. He was rather thin and spotty, with a long nose, and bandy legs, and nasty unpolished plywood teeth, and a rare foot disease, but, thought Mitzi, a prince is a prince, and she fell in love with him without another thought.

And after a time, or a few times anyway, he, too, fell in love with her, and a few hours later they were on their way to ask King Otto's permission to wed, as this latest prince didn't read the newspapers any more than any of the others did, decadent, dimwitted, parasitic little bastards that they were.

'Is he in the book?' asked the King, surlily.

'Yes, Daddy,' cried Princess Mitzi, delightedly.

'Do you love my daughter?' queried the wise old King.

'Could be,' allowed Prince Walter, nasally.

'Do you,' continued the wise old King, 'want her hand in marriage?'

An uneasy silence fell upon the assembled courtiers, for none of them much cared for Walter's looks, not even the Lord Chancellor, who was extremely gay.

'. . . Yeah, all right.'

'In that case,' said the King, 'I must set you a task to prove you worthy of my daughter's hand.'

'Why?' came the bold reply.

'Because she's a fuckin' Princess, that's why,' explained the King, scarcely controlling his rage. 'And your task is that you must, quite unaided and unarmed, go down the town and get me twenty Marlboro.'

'What, now!?' exploded Walter.

'Not necessarily,' cried the King weakly, smiling round the court with all the easy spontaneity of a chat show host, 'I'll think about it.'

(To be continued.)

MR CHEEKY

NISUS WETTUS: Next? Crucifixion?

FIRST PRISONER: Yes.

NISUS WETTUS: Good . . . right. Out of the door, line on the left, one cross each . . . next . . . Crucifixion?

SECOND PRISONER: Yes.

NISUS WETTUS: Good . . . Out of the door, line on the left, one cross each . . . Next? Crucifixion?

MR CHEEKY: Er . . . no . . . freedom . . .

NISUS WETTUS: What?

MR CHEEKY: Er . . . freedom for me . . . They said I hadn't done anything so I could go free and live on an island somewhere.

NISUS WETTUS: Well, that's jolly good . . . In that case . . .

(*he goes to strike out Mr Cheeky's name*)

MR CHEEKY: No . . . no . . . it's crucifixion really. Just pulling your leg.

NISUS WETTUS: Oh . . . I see. Very good . . . out of the door, line on the . . .

MR CHEEKY: Yes . . . I know the way . . . out the door, line on the left, one cross each.

ALWAYS LOOK ON THE BRIGHT SIDE OF LIFE

MR CHEEKY: Cheer up, Brian. You know what they say . . .

Some things in life are bad

They can really make you mad

Other things just make you swear and curse.

When you're chewing on life's gristle

Don't grumble, give a whistle

And this'll help things turn out for the best . . .

And . . .

Always look on the bright side of life . . . (*whistle*)

Always look on the light side of life . . . (*whistle*)

If life seems jolly rotten

There's something you've forgotten

And that's to laugh and smile and dance and sing,

When you're feeling in the dumps,

Don't be silly chumps,

Just purse your lips and whistle – that's the thing.

And . . . always look on the bright side of life . . . (*whistle*)

Come on. (*others start to join in*)

Always look on the right side of life . . . (*whistle*)

For life is quite absurd

And death's the final word

You must always face the curtain with a bow.

Forget about your sin – give the audience a grin

Enjoy it – it's your last chance anyhow.

So . . . always look on the bright side of death
Just before you draw your terminal breath.
Life's a piece of shit
When you look at it,
Life's a laugh and death's a joke, it's true,
You'll see it's all a show,
Keep 'em laughing as you go
Just remember that the last laugh is on you.
And . . . always look on the bright side of life . . . (*whistle*)
Always look on the right side of life . . . (*etc*).

FOREWORD BY THE LATE
GRAHAM CHAPMAN

Sorry this foreword is a bit late. You can get a bit behind in the after life. There's so much time here it takes an eternity to do anything.

Many people go completely quiet after they are dead. But not me. In fact in the last few years I have released more books and records than the rest of the Pythons put together, and they aren't even dead yet. Mind you, that Cleese looked a bit frail last time I saw him on TV. Has he had some kind of facial work? And dear old Mickey Palin was looking a bit florid. All that travelling can't be good for him, and he was always a bit fond of the old Bordeaux. Gilliam has qualified for his bus pass and Jonesy looks quite decrepit. I'm told he can't even remember which one he was.

In fact only Eric Idle looks at all decent. I always fancied him. He was certainly the nicest of the lot. I miss him the most. I'm glad to see he has put together a selection of some of the gags and skits which once so amused the Nation. Fortunately tastes have matured over the years and so this sort of collection seems incredibly dated and certainly déja-vu all over again. But *Futuaris Nisi Irrisus Ridebis*, as we say up here. Fuck 'em if they can't take a joke.

Well, got to dash. A Mr Heisenberg is going to explain his Uncertainty Theory to God, which should be quite interesting as we are still unsure whether He exists or not. And they call this closure!

Love to you all,
Graham 'Doc' Chapman

INDEX